21st Century Skills Library

REAL WORLD MATH: PERSONAL FINANCE

SAVING FOR THE FUTURE

Cecilia Minden

Cherry Lake Publishing
Ann Arbor, Michigan

Published in the United States of America by Cherry Lake Publishing
Ann Arbor, MI
www.cherrylakepublishing.com

Math Education Adviser: Timothy J. Whiteford, PhD, Associate Professor of Education, St. Michael's College, Colchester, Vermont

Finance Adviser: Ryan Spaude, CFP®, Kitchenmaster Financial Services, LLC, North Mankato, Minnesota

Photo Credits: Cover and page 1, © Sean Justice, Corbis

Library of Congress Cataloging-in-Publication Data
Minden, Cecilia.
  Saving for the future / by Cecilia Minden.
    p. cm. — (Real world math)
  ISBN-13: 978-1-60279-001-8
  ISBN-10: 1-60279-001-9
  1. Finance, Personal—Juvenile literature. 2. Saving and investment—Juvenile literature. I. Title.
II. Series.
  HG179.M5256 2008
  332.6—dc22   2007006386

*Cherry Lake Publishing would like to acknowledge the work of
The Partnership for 21st Century Skills.
Please visit www.21stcenturyskills.org for more information.*

TABLE OF CONTENTS

CHAPTER ONE

WHY SAVE MONEY?

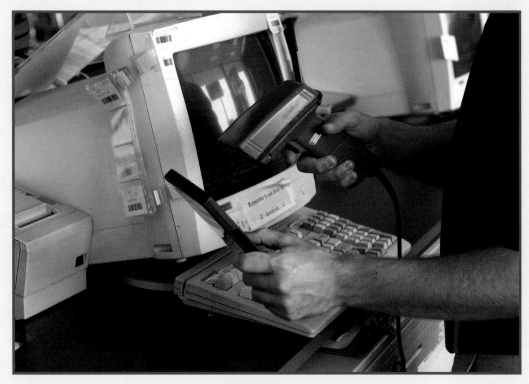

Do you go to the store and spend your money as soon as you get it?

Do you get money from an allowance or a job? Do you spend every last cent before the week is out? Lots of kids spend it all right away. Lots of adults do, too.

Sooner or later, most people discover that saving money is the smart thing to do. Having savings can help you deal with unexpected events. Maybe you have been saving up to buy a sweater that you saw at your favorite store. Today you were invited to a party and want something new to wear. Your parents tell you that you have plenty of things to wear in your closet, but that you are welcome to buy something new with your own money. If you have savings, you can pay for the unexpected clothes expense as well as the planned future costs.

People don't just save for the unexpected. They also save to reach financial goals. You might want to buy an expensive bike. Maybe you need a new pair of jeans. Either way, it is going to cost more money than you receive as your weekly allowance. You'll probably want to save for both short-term and long-term goals. For example, you want to take your dad

Saving up to buy a car is a long-term goal.

to a movie for his birthday. His birthday is in two weeks. You have to save

money to pay for movie tickets, popcorn, candy, and drinks. This is a

short-term goal.

Other short-term goals might be buying a video game, a CD, or a new camera. Maybe your short-term goal is a concert or sporting event ticket. With short-term goals, you can save the money you need within a few weeks or months.

Long-term goals are more expensive items. You need more time to save more money. Maybe you are already saving to pay for college or a car. These are long-term goals.

You need to put aside money to reach your short- and long-term goals. Are you saving as much as you can right now? If you aren't, how can you change your ways? Let's find out!

Learning & Innovation Skills

You're standing on the sidewalk staring in the window of a store called Hair's to You! Laid out before your eyes is a rainbow of clips and headbands, scrunchies and ties. Your eye falls on an elegant headband made of shimmering blue and green beads. It's only $4.00! Why not buy it?

When you see something you would like to buy, always ask yourself, "Do I need it, or do I want it?" When you satisfy a *need*, you complete a goal. When you satisfy a *want*, you fulfill a temporary urge. Do you need another headband? You have a dozen at home, so you probably don't need it, no matter how beautiful it is.

It is hard to make choices, but you have to, in order to save money. Buy what you need, and save the rest for your short- and long-term goals.

CHAPTER TWO

STRATEGIES FOR SAVING

Small amounts of money can add up to big savings over time.

Saving money doesn't have to be difficult, but it does take effort. You have to decide to do it. There are some simple strategies you can use to help yourself save money.

First, determine how much you want to save. Make a list of your weekly expenses. Look at the list, and decide what you need and what you can do without. This will help you figure out just how

REAL WORLD MATH CHALLENGE

Jacob decides to save 15 percent of all the money he receives each week. Last week, he received a gift of $30.00 for his birthday, $6.00 for his allowance, and $9.00 for cleaning up his neighbor's yard. **How much money did Jacob take in that week? How much did he put into savings? How much would he put into savings if he was saving 25 percent of his money?**

(Turn to page 29 for the answers)

much you can set aside for savings. Try to come up with a percentage rather than a dollar amount. That way, if you get some extra money one week, you'll save even more.

Take the money you're planning to save out of your allowance as soon as you receive it. Don't let yourself be swayed by thoughts of "just this week" or "just this one time." Put that money in a bank or someplace where you can't get to it easily. Making regular deposits in a savings account is one of the best habits you can have.

Using a nearby automated teller machine (ATM) can make it convenient to make regular deposits in a savings account.

How can you hold on to the rest of your allowance? Planning ahead can help to keep you from spending it. Imagine you are going to the mall today with your friends. Whenever you go to the mall, you always buy a big cookie. Today, why not take along a piece of fruit or a bag of trail mix instead? That way, you'll save some money—*and* you'll eat a healthier snack!

Did you find a great shirt at the mall? Rather than buying it right away, wait a day. You don't have to worry that someone else will buy it. Most retail stores will hold an item for you for 24 hours. This gives you time to think about a purchase and to decide whether you *want* it or really *need* it. If you still want to buy the item the next day, you need to come up with a plan for how you will pay for it.

You've decided to save up for a snowboard. You're putting aside a percentage of your money every week. How do you know if you'll have enough money to buy the snowboard by the time winter comes? You have to do the math!

CHAPTER THREE

Do the Math: How Long Will It Take?

Saving for a goal takes patience. As you're waiting for your savings to grow, try to stay positive. Don't think, "It will take forever to save enough money." Instead, remind yourself that each day you are closer to your goal

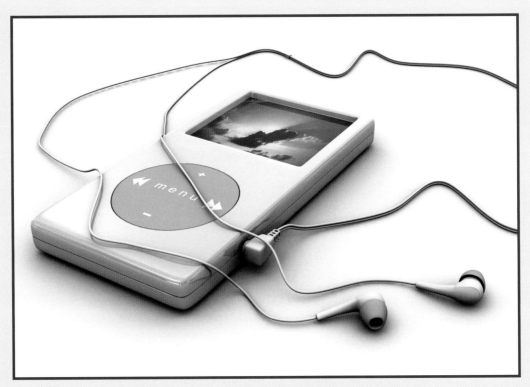

How long do you think it would take you to save
enough money to buy a new MP3 Player?

12

21st CENTURY SKILLS LIBRARY

than you were yesterday or last week or last year. If you don't keep your goal in mind, you're much more likely to let down your guard and spend money you had been planning on saving.

When making a short-term or a long-term goal, it's important to figure out how long it will take to achieve it. Knowing how long it will take will help you focus on the goal.

21st Century Content

Managing your money requires you to set spending goals and priorities and then work toward them. Using a calendar may help you keep on track for accomplishing your goals.

Draw or paste a picture of what you want to buy on the date you want to buy it. You could even paper clip your money to the pages. Then, if you are tempted to use that money on something else, you will be reminded of your goal.

REAL WORLD MATH CHALLENGE

Carmen wants to buy an MP3 player. She has picked out one that costs $79.00 plus 7 percent sales tax. **What is the total cost of the MP3 player?**

Carmen's grandparents gave her $50.00 for her birthday to put toward the cost of the MP3 player she wants. Her allowance is $8.00 a week. She is saving $4.00 a week from her allowance. **How long will it take for Carmen to save enough money to buy the MP3 player?**

(Turn to page 29 for the answers)

You can open a savings account at a local bank.

With long-term goals, you have time to seek out more ways to make and save money. A good way to increase your buying power is to open a savings account. The bank will pay you for letting them keep your money. The money you earn is called interest. When your money is earning interest, your money makes money *for* you.

Let's say you have $500 and want to open a savings account. You put your money in an account earning 5 percent interest. At the end of one year, you will have $525—your original $500 plus $25 in interest. At the end of two years, you will have $551.25. That's the $525 plus $26.25 in interest. Why did you get more interest the second year? Because you earned interest on the interest you made the first year! With interest, not only does your money make money, but the amount of money it makes increases each year.

Talk to your parents about helping you set up a savings account. Do research to find out where you can earn the highest rate of interest on your money.

Tim just turned 11 years old. He wants to save money so he can buy a used car when he turns 16. He gets a weekly allowance of $7.00. When he turns 12, he will get $9.00 a week. When he turns 14, he will get $12.00 a week. He plans to save 50 percent of his allowance each week. **How much money will he have in 5 years?**

When he turns 16, Tim decides to wait and buy a car when he goes to college at age 18. Now he puts all the money he saved for the car into an account earning 10 percent interest. **How much will he have at age 18?**

(Turn to page 29 for the answers)

Remember that snowboard you wanted? You did the math and figured out that it will take you six months to save enough money to buy it. But it's already September! By the time you get the board, winter will be over. How can you save more?

CHAPTER FOUR

DO THE MATH:
HOW CAN I SAVE MORE?

You can use any kind of small notebook to keep a money diary.

Have you heard anyone say, "Money just slips through my fingers"? Do

you know where your money goes? To find out, try an experiment.

For two weeks, keep a money diary. Keep a small notebook with you

in your pocket or backpack at all times. Write down everything, absolutely

Some people spend a lot of money ordering pizza and other snacks.

everything, that you buy and the cost of each item.

No amount is too small to include. At the end of

the two weeks, total up the costs. How much did

you spend? What do you have to show for it? Look

over your list. Divide the items into these categories: food, clothing, school, and other. Did you spend most of your money on snacks? Are there a lot of items listed under "other"? Were these items things that you wanted or needed? Keeping track of how you spend your money will help you see ways to save.

Buying toys and other things that you want
but don't need can quickly add up.

Now that you have a money diary, you can get a better handle on where

to cut expenses. Eating out is a category in which it is easy to spend too

much money. Bring snacks from home instead. You can also cut expenses

Doing extra chores, such as washing your family's
car, may be one way to earn extra money.

by shopping at sales and using coupons. Put the money you save into your savings account.

What if you've cut expenses but still need more money to reach your goals? Then you need to find ways to earn extra money.

Start by offering to do extra chores around the house. A good place to begin is by thinking about your regular chores. If your job is feeding the dog, maybe you could also brush, wash, and walk the dog. Once you've come up with a list of jobs, try to figure out what you think would be a fair payment for each. Next you'll need to present your list and the prices to your parents. Choose a time when they are not busy doing other things. Negotiate a price that you all agree is fair.

You might also want to take your job list around to your neighbors. Offer to do the same jobs for them. Maybe they will have other jobs they want you to do. Keep a professional attitude. Show up on time, be polite,

clean up afterward, and thank them for the work. If you make a good

impression, they will hire you again. And they will recommend you to

their friends. Now you're running your own business!

REAL WORLD MATH CHALLENGE

Carmen's friend Amy also wants to buy the MP3 player that costs $79.00 plus 7 percent tax. She has $25.00 saved already. Amy wants to buy her MP3 player in one month (4 weeks). By cutting back on the money she spends on food, she is now saving $4.50 a week.

Amy asked her neighbors if she could babysit for them for $3.00 an hour. Mrs. Michaels hired her for 3 hours a week for 2 weeks. Mrs. Lambert hired her for 2 hours a week for 4 weeks. **Will Amy have enough money to buy the MP3 player at the end of 4 weeks?**

(Turn to page 29 for the answer)

CHAPTER FIVE

PLANNING FOR THE FUTURE

*Saving up to buy a new piece of clothing is
usually a short-term savings goal.*

Most people have both short-term goals and long-term goals. Your

favorite cousin is getting married next month and you want to buy a

gift to take to the wedding. That's a short-term goal. There is also a truly awesome guitar in the window of Mike's Music Shop. That's a long-term goal. How do you accomplish both goals? You need to plan for the future.

The best way to do this is to create a savings plan. Deciding how much to save each week is great. But if you want to achieve a variety of goals, you should also think about how you want to divide that savings up. Split the amount you save into different categories. These categories might include saving for long-term goals, saving for short-term goals, saving money to donate to your favorite charity, and saving money to spend freely. Set aside a percentage of your savings for each of the categories.

REAL WORLD MATH CHALLENGE

Joey has an allowance of $8.00 a week. He decides to create a savings plan. He will give 15 percent of his money to charity. He will save 20 percent for long-term goals and 30 percent for short-term goals. The remaining 35 percent is his to spend as he wants. **How much money goes into each category each week?**

(Turn to page 29 for the answer)

Keep another record of different short- and long-term goals. Write down the prices for each goal. Keep track of what you've saved toward each goal. Your chart might look something like this:

Short-term Goal	Price	Money Saved
New video game	$19.95	
DVD	$17.99	
Long-term Goal	Price	
Vacation money	$250	
New drum set	$399	

If you keep close tabs on your progress, you're more likely to meet your goals. You need to set up a plan that works for you. Some people use a computer program to help them keep their money organized. Whether your plan is on paper or on the computer, the important thing is that you have a plan and you use it.

Life & Career Skills

Not everyone has the money to pay for basic needs such as food, clothing, and shelter. Charities collect donations to help care for people in need, both close to home and around the world. Maybe you want to donate money to help victims of an earthquake in Pakistan. Or perhaps you want to give money to help people in a shelter for the homeless in your hometown. Choose a charity that means something to you. Make regular donations. Your money will be put to good use.

Knowing how to manage money will give you a sense of accomplishment. Spending money wisely will give you confidence. These are skills that will help you the rest of your life. It is fun to look at all the different things you can buy. It is exciting to

Volunteering your time is another good way to help your favorite charity.

If you keep track of the money you receive and the money you spend,
you'll be well on your way to figuring out the best savings plan for you.

think about owning them. But it takes practice to make good decisions

about the right things to buy. With a little planning and research, your

money can go a long way. Instead of being broke, you'll buy things that

you care about. Your money will be working for you.

If you make a savings plan and stick to it, your money will go a long way!

REAL WORLD MATH CHALLENGE ANSWERS

Chapter Two

Page 9

Jacob received $45.00 in one week.

$30.00 + $6.00 + $9.00 = $45

If Jacob saves 15 percent, he will put $6.75 into savings. If he saves 25 percent, he will put $11.25 into savings.

$45.00 x 0.15 = $6.75

$45.00 x 0.25 = $11.25

Chapter Three

Page 13

The tax on the MP3 player is $5.53. The total cost of the MP3 player, including tax, is $84.53.

$79.00 x 0.07 = $5.53

$79.00 + $5.53 = $84.53

After her birthday, Carmen still needs $34.53.

$84.53 – $50.00 = $34.53

She can save $34.53 in 9 weeks.

$34.53 ÷ $4.00 = 9 weeks (8.6 rounded up to 9)

Page 16

By saving 50 percent of his allowance each week, Tim will save $182.00 at age 11.

50% of $7.00 = 0.50 x $7.00 = $3.50

$3.50 x 52 (weeks in a year) = $182.00

Tim will save a total of $468.00 at ages 12 and 13.

50% of $9.00 = 0.50 x $9.00 = $4.50

$4.50 x 52 x 2 = $468.00

Tim will save a total of $624.00 at ages 14 and 15.

50% of $12.00 = 0.50 x $12.00 = $6.00

$6.00 x 52 x 2 = $624.00

Tim has $1,274.00 on his 16th birthday.

$182.00 + $468.00 + $624.00 = $1,274

At age 17, Tim has $1,401.40.

10% of $1,274.00 = 0.10 x $1,274.00 = $127.40

$1,274.00 + $127.40 = $1,401.40

Tim's total savings at age 18 is $1,541.54.

10% of $1,401.40 = 0.10 x $1,401.40 = $140.14

$1,401.40 + $140.14 = $1,541.54

Chapter Four

Page 22

The total cost of the MP3 player is $84.53.

7% of $79.00 = 0.07 x $79.00 = $5.53

$79.00 + $5.53 = $84.53

Amy needs to save $59.53 more to buy the MP3 player.

$84.53 – $25.00 = $59.53

In 4 weeks, Amy will save $18.00 from her allowance.

$4.50 x 4 = $18.00

Amy will earn $18.00 babysitting for Mrs. Michaels and $24.00 babysitting for Mrs. Lambert.

$3.00 x 3 hours x 2 weeks = $18.00

$3.00 x 2 hours x 4 weeks = $24.00

Yes, Amy will be able to buy the MP3 player after 4 weeks.

$18.00 + $18.00 + $24.00 = $60.00

Chapter Five

Page 24

Each week, Joey will give $1.20 to charity. He will save $1.60 for long-term goals and $2.40 for short-term goals. He has $2.80 to spend as he wants.

15% = $8.00 x 0.15 = $1.20

20% = $8.00 x 0.20 = $1.60

30% = $8.00 x 0.30 = $2.40

35% = $8.00 x 0.35 = $2.80

Glossary

charity (CHEHR-uh-tee) an organization to help the needy, or a gift to such an organization

coupons (KOO-ponz) pieces of paper that give you discounts on purchases

deposits (dih-PAW-zutz) amounts of money put in a bank

interest (IN-tuh-rest) the amount earned on money kept in a bank

negotiate (nih-GO-shee-ate) to talk over something with others and reach an agreement

FOR MORE INFORMATION

Books

Harmon, Hollis Page. *Money Sense for Kids*. Hauppauge, NY: Barron's, 2004.

Heckman, Philip. *Saving Money (How Economics Works)*. Minneapolis: Lerner, 2006.

Holyoke, Nancy. *A Smart Girl's Guide to Money: How to Make It, Save It, and Spend It*. Middleton, WI: American Girl, 2006.

Web Sites

Hands on Banking
www.handsonbanking.org/
For an interactive program that teaches banking and money management skills

Kids.gov: Money
www.kids.gov/k_money.htm
Links to many government sites with information on money and banking for kids

PBS: It's My Life
pbskids.org/itsmylife/money/managing/article7.html
Money management information and games

INDEX

ABOUT THE AUTHOR

Cecilia Minden, PhD, is a literacy consultant and the author of many books for children. She is the former director of the Language and Literacy Program at Harvard Graduate School of Education in Cambridge, Massachusetts. She would like to thank fifth-grade math teacher Beth Rottinghaus for her help with the Real World Math Challenges. Cecilia lives with her family in North Carolina.